You Can Draw

Cars

SALARIYA

Published in Great Britain in MMXII by
Book House, an imprint of
The Salariya Book Company Ltd
25 Marlborough Place, Brighton BN1 1UB

1 3 5 7 9 8 6 4 2

Please visit our websites at **www.salariya.com** or
www.book-house.co.uk for **free** electronic versions of:
You Wouldn't Want to Be an Egyptian Mummy!
You Wouldn't Want to Be a Roman Gladiator!
You Wouldn't Want to be a Polar Explorer!
**You Wouldn't Want to Sail on a 19th-Century
Whaling Ship!**

Author: Mark Bergin was born in Hastings in 1961. He
studied at Eastbourne College of Art and has specialised
in historical reconstructions as well as aviation and
maritime subjects since 1983. He lives in Bexhill-on-
Sea with his wife and three children.

Editor: Rob Walker

PB ISBN: 978-1-908759-52-8

A CIP catalogue record for this book is available from
the British Library.

Printed and bound in China.
Printed on paper from sustainable sources.

Visit our **new** online shop at
shop.salariya.com
for great offers, gift ideas, all our new releases

and free postage and packaging.

PAPER FROM
SUSTAINABLE
FORESTS

You Can Draw

Cars

By Mark Bergin

Contents

Introduction

Learning to draw is fun. In this book a finished drawing will be broken up into stages as a guide to completing your own drawing. However, this is only the beginning. The more you practise, the better you will get. Have fun coming up with cool designs, adding more incredible details and using new materials to achieve different effects!

This is an example showing how each drawing will be built up in easy stages. New sections of drawing will be shown in colour to make each additional step clear.

1

2

3

4

5

With practice, you too will be
able to draw cars just like these
examples shown here.

Materials

There are many different art materials available which you can use to draw and colour in your cars. Try out each one for new and exciting results. The more you practise with them, the better your drawing skills will get!

Use a pencil to draw the shape of your car. Any mistakes you make can easily be erased, as can any construction lines that are left over at the end of your drawing.

An eraser can be used to rub out any pencil mistakes. It can also be used to create highlights on pencil drawings.

You can go over your finished pencil lines with pen to make the lines bolder. But remember, a pen line is permanent so you can't erase any mistakes!

Coloured pencils come in a huge range of colours and can be layered over each other for new and exciting effects.

Pastels can be smudged and blended together to give you all sorts of different effects.

Felt tip pens can add vibrant colour to your drawing. But remember that they are hard to layer and the colour is permanent so you can't make any mistakes!

9

Inspiration

Many types of cars are made throughout the world. You can choose any of them for the inspiration for your cartoon-style drawing. Photos, magazines or books can give you new ideas and new designs to try.

When turning your car into a cartoon-style, two-dimensional drawing, concentrate on the key elements you want to include and the overall shape of the car.

One way to make your car look cool is to make it a lot shorter in length and make the wheels a lot bigger.

Use new colours and designs to make your car look the way you want it to. It's your drawing after all.

VW Beetle

The VW Beetle is one of the world's best-known cars. There have been over 20 million produced worldwide.

Draw two circles for the wheels. Add an overlapping rectangle for the body.

Add curves for the bonnet, roof and rear end.

Draw in the front and back bumpers and the wheel arches.

Add two more circles inside each of the wheels. These will be the hubcaps.

Draw in the windows, door handle and wing mirror. Add front and rear lights.

Finish your Beetle by colouring the bodywork. Finish off any leftover details.

13

Bugatti

The Bugatti type 35 was a very successful racing car in the 1920s. It won many Grand Prix races in its time.

Draw two ovals for the wheels, with an overlapping rectangle for the body.

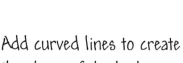

Add curved lines to create the shape of the body.

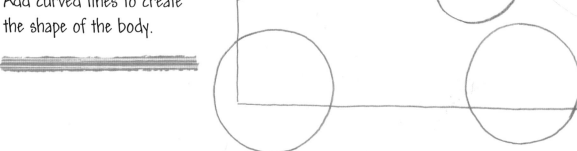

Draw in two circles for the inner wheel and add a spare wheel strapped to the middle of the body.

Draw in vents for the engine and add other small details.

Draw in the driver and add the hubcaps.

Colour in your drawing, adding finishing touches like the racing number.

Saleen S7

The Saleen S7 is a very fast road and racing car. The race version has competed in GT championships and at Le Mans.

Draw two circles for wheels and add a box shape with a sloping top for the body.

Draw in curved lines to make the shape of the bonnet, roof and rear end.

Add the windows and inner circles for the hubcaps.

Draw in the large side air vents and a wing mirror.

Add all of the remaining small details to the car, such as lights and a rear spoiler.

Finish off your Saleen racing car by adding colour to the different sections.

Dragster

These cars are designed to compete in straight-line races over a quarter mile (about 400 metres). They run on special fuel and are designed to accelerate incredibly fast.

Draw two circles for the wheels; one small, one large. Add the overlapping sloped body shape.

Add an inner circle on each wheel and draw in the driver's seat and the shape of the engine.

Add the driver and the roll bar.

Add the front spoiler, the engine intake and a rear spoiler.

Draw in the wheel details, the exhaust pipes and the rear framework.

Colour in your dragster, adding a racing number and design of your own!

24

Chrysler

This family car has cool retro styling but has all the features of a modern car.

Start your drawing with two circles and add a deep box shape for the main body.

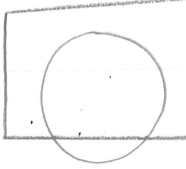

Draw in curves for the body shape. Add the roof and two inner circles for the wheels.

Draw in the roof frame, front and back bumpers and add circles for the hubcaps.

Draw in the windows
and the wing mirror.

Draw in the doors and
handles, the wheel arches,
the headlights and the tail
lights.

Add any remaining details and finish your
drawing by colouring it in.

Cadillac

This classic American car has a really eye-catching shape with massive tail fins at its rear.

Draw two circles for the wheels and add a rectangle for the body.

Add curves for the bonnet, the roof and a large tail fin.

Draw in the door and windows. Add the bumper and two lines at the rear of the car.

Draw in the front and rear lights. Add the front grill and draw the wheel arches at different levels.

Add small details to the windows and side of the car. Add more circles to the wheels for the hubcaps.

Finish off your Cadillac by colouring in your drawing and adding any small design details.

Nascar

The NASCAR (National Association for Stock Car Auto Racing) vehicle is an American track car built for fast and exciting racing.

Draw in two circles for the wheels and add a long oblong box shape for the body.

Draw in the shape of the car's roof and the bonnet dipping inside the box.

Add the front and rear bumpers and the base of the windows. Add a curve to the front bonnet.

Draw in the windows, a small spoiler and add the curved wheel arches.

Draw in the front and rear lights. Add more circles within the wheels. Draw in the final small details.

Finish off your drawing by adding colour and details like sponsorship stickers and the racing number.

25

Hot Rod

These super-charged street racers are custom built and raced by their owners.

Draw two circles for wheels and add a rectangle shape that is higher at the back.

Add lines for the roof and doors.

Add curves to the body shape and draw in the wheel arches.

Position the window high in the top section of the car. Add the large engine and the front and rear lights to the car body.

Draw circles within the wheels for the hubcaps. Add lines to the body, and an exhaust.

Finish adding the details of the car and then colour it in. Don't forget the awesome fire design down the side of the car!

Formula 1

The fastest racing is found in Formula 1. These cars are designed to cut through the air and can reach speeds of 355 kph.

Draw two circles for the wheels and add a sloped box shape for the body.

Add circles within the wheels and a squared-off frame at the rear of the car.

Draw in the front and rear spoiler shapes. Add the driver's helmet.

Add more details to the driver's helmet. Draw in lines on the spoilers. Add another small circle in the centre of each wheel.

Finish the front spoiler. Add the air intakes on the side. Finish off any remaining details.

Colour in your Formula 1 car, adding any remaining details and designs you want. Now you're ready for a race!

More views

For an extra drawing challenge try drawing your cars from the front or rear! Practising different views will help you improve your drawing.

Back View

Mini Cooper

Start with two rectangles for the wheels.

Add another rectangle for the car body then add the rear window.

Draw in the roof, rear lights, number plate and bumper. Add curves to both sides of the car.

Finish off any details. A pencil has been used to draw and add tone to this example. Try other materials to create a different look.

Front View

Start with two rectangles for the wheels. Add two smaller rectangles as shown.

Draw two bigger, overlapping rectangles for the main body of the car.

Draw in the windows. Add the front lights, the grill and the bonnet shapes.

Finish the front view of the car by adding extra details. Then either add colour or just add pencil tone as shown.

31

Glossary

bodywork The body of the car.

bonnet Hinged cover over the engine of a vehicle.

construction lines Guidelines used in the early stages of a drawing. They are usually erased later.

engine intake A metal tube that's part of the engine of a powerful vehicle.

framework The solid frame that holds the car together and gives it its shape.

grill A series of slits in the bodywork, near the car's engine, which help hot air escape.

hubcap A metal covering that clips onto the side of a wheel.

roll bar A safety bar featured in racing vehicles. It protects the driver's head in case of a crash.

spoiler A part of the car's design that allows air to flow over the car smoothly.

vent Similar to a grill, but down the side of the car.

wheel arches Arches of metal that protect the tops of the wheels.

Index